For Mike and Leo Barton, my very favorite humans.
Also for Rebecca Rivera, Sustainable Fashion Designer
and Intersectional Environmentalist, for continually teaching
and inspiring me to consider my impact on our planet.

Special thanks to Dr. Libby Ellwood, Ph.D.
Her work is at the intersection of conservation, climate change,
community science, and educating the public. (All the cool stuff!)
I'm inspired by what she's doing, and she was kind enough
to let me consult her on this book (during a pandemic, even!).

VIKING
An imprint of Penguin Random House LLC, New York

First published in the United States of America by Viking, an imprint of Penguin Random House LLC, 2021

Visit us online at penguinrandomhouse.com.

LIBRARY OF CONGRESS CATALOGING-IN-PUBLICATION DATA IS AVAILABLE.

Manufactured in China

ISBN 9780593207031

10 9 8 7 6 5 4 3

The artwork in this book was created using ink and Beam Handmade Watercolor paints (which are sustainable and altogether rad) on paper, alongside Photoshop CC. The main text was lettered with a well-loved bamboo calligraphy pen and ink. Innumerable cups of tea were consumed in the process.

Yum! Sometimes termites eat books.

I'M TRYING to LOVE GARBAGE

WORDS & PICTURES by bethany bARTon

VIKING

HI! I'm the VOICE OF
YOUR FRIENDLY NEIGHBORHOOD
NARRATOR, HERE to TALK ABOUT
ANOTHER EXCITING TOPIC.

AND THIS TIME It's...

We're NATURE'S garbage collectors!

Thankfully, nature has a pretty sweet system going on, with food chains making sure living organisms use each other for food and energy.

PRODUCERS like plants create their own energy

plant

Who are then consumed by TERTIARY CONSUMERS

snake

frog

Who get eaten up by SECONDARY CONSUMERS

Who are gobbled up by APEX PREDATORS at the top of the food chain

owl

They get eaten up by PRIMARY CONSUMERS

grasshopper

But once we get to the end of the food chain... it's not over yet!

YIKES!

THAT STUFF STINKS!

CAN WE WAVE THAT
SMELL OUTTA HERE?

QUICK! GRAB THE PAGE AND
WAVE IT BACK AND FORTH
UNTIL THAT STINK GOES AWAY!

DECOMPOSERS

DETRITIVORES

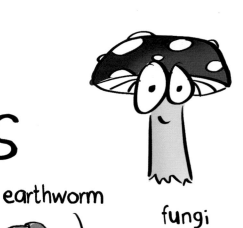
fungi

bacteria

fly

earthworm

fiddler crab

dung beetle

We're the critters that eat and process nature's leftovers so nothing goes to waste.

WAIT...

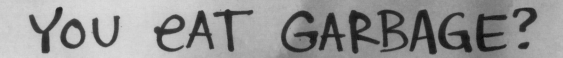

SCAVENGERS are creatures that feed on carrion (a fancy word for dead animals), dead plants, and other trash for all their food!

Vultures almost never hunt. Instead they eat up dead animals they find.

Rats and cockroaches are scavengers you can find even in urban areas.

Termites are scavengers that prefer to eat deadwood.

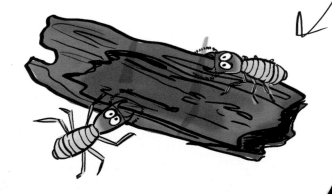

I THINK I'M GOING TO BARF.

DETRITIVORE is a fancy word for trash eater.

When we use that word, we are usually referring to a creature that feeds on dead organic material, especially dead plants.

Earthworms eat dead plants, animal waste, and dirt, and then poop out better dirt. Seriously!

DECOMPOSERS are organisms that break down the waste and remains of living things.

Which means detritivores are decomposers too!

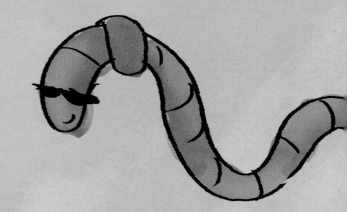

But while detritivores have to eat dead organic material to break it down, decomposers like fungi and bacteria have a different trick!

fungi

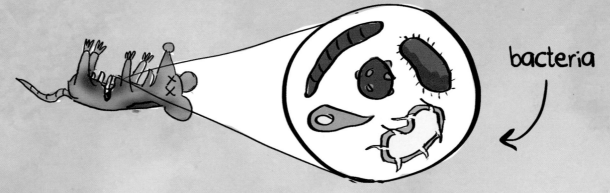

bacteria

They release special chemicals called enzymes to break down the decaying material, and then absorb any nutrients!

Detritivores and decomposers are on cleanup duty in the ocean too!

Fiddler crabs sift through sand to find algae and decaying plants.

Sea cucumbers eat algae and the poop from other ocean creatures (eww).

Some decomposers even help clean water.

In wetlands, microorganisms can absorb nutrients, helping to filter mucky water.

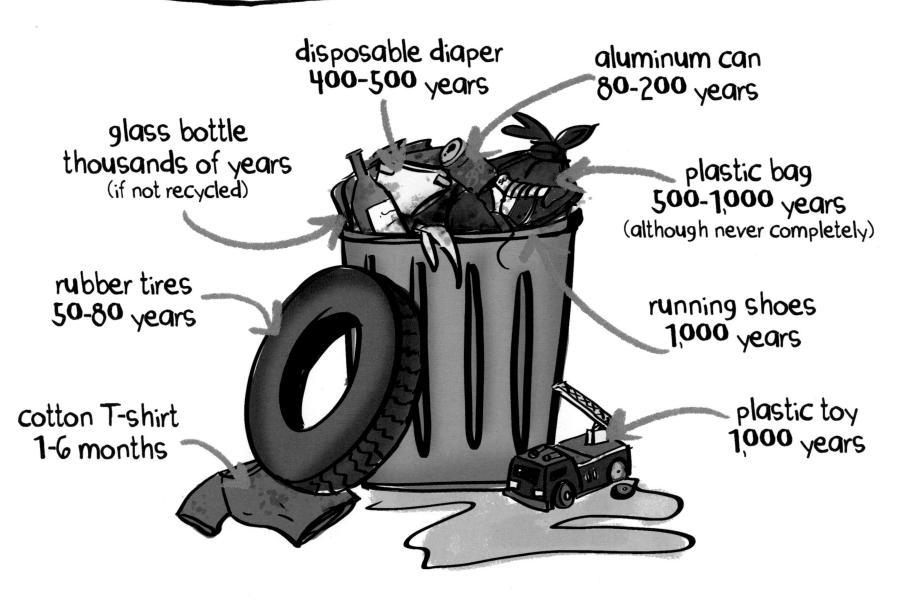

While organic waste can be broken down by critters like us, most inorganic waste can't. And it takes MUCH longer to break down.

disposable diaper
400-500 years

aluminum can
80-200 years

glass bottle
thousands of years
(if not recycled)

plastic bag
500-1,000 years
(although never completely)

rubber tires
50-80 years

running shoes
1,000 years

cotton T-shirt
1-6 months

plastic toy
1,000 years

1,000 YEARS? WHERE DO WE PUT STUFF FOR 1,000 YEARS?!

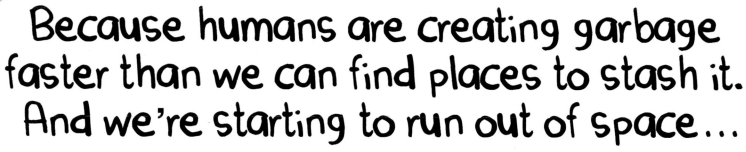

REDUCE means to use less!

Find new uses for containers and cans!

You can carry a reusable water bottle instead of buying new plastic ones!

Swap toys, books, or clothes you don't use with friends. Or donate for someone else to use!

Mend clothing rather than buying something new!

REUSE items! Give them a new home or a new purpose instead of trashing them!

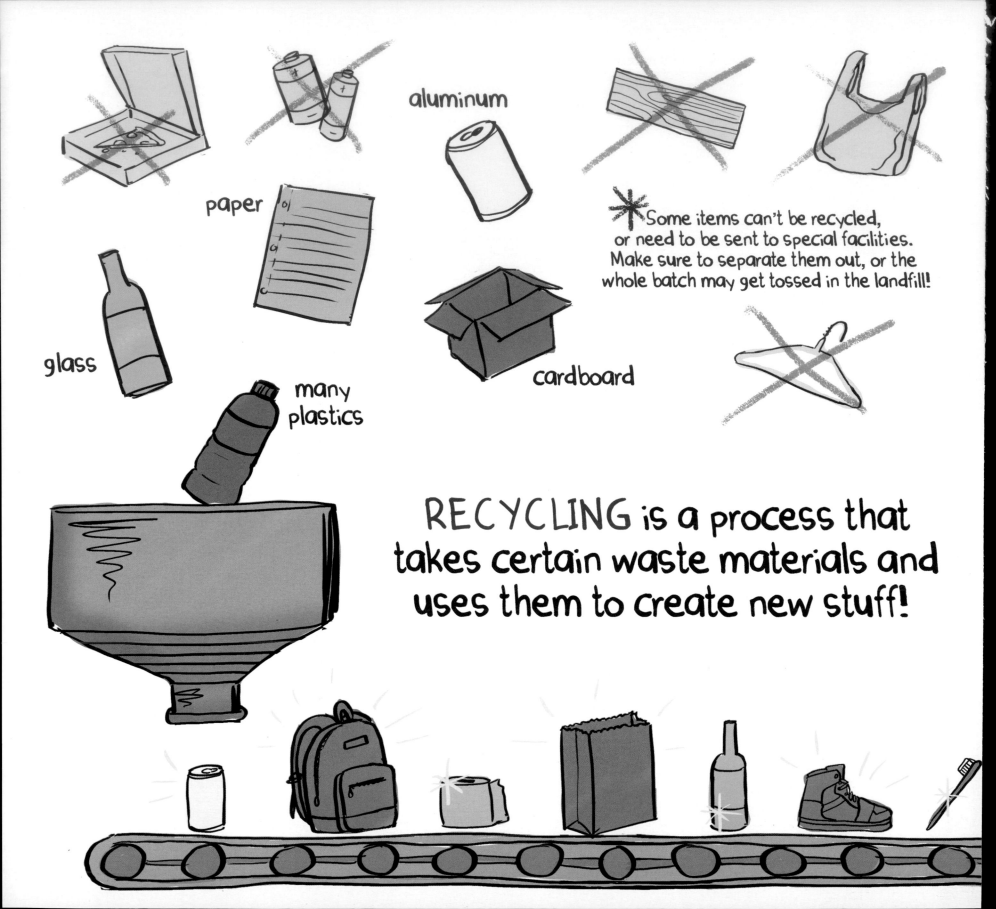

You can even reduce and reuse your organic trash at home by making COMPOST!

This will make us microorganisms really happy!

Mix food scraps from fruits and veggies with equal parts yard waste (like dead leaves) and a bit of dirt. You don't need a special container! A bucket with a lid or even a sturdy trash bag will do.

COMPOST

With time, you will have created fancy new dirt (called compost) that plants and flowers love!

THAT'S REALLY COOL, BUT THE BOOK IS ALMOST OVER. AND I DON'T LOVE GARBAGE YET.

BUT I DO WANT TO ACT MORE LIKE YOU GUYS...

AND EAT GARBAGE?

Yay! Dig in!

NO, NO... GROSS.

I MEANT I WANT to ACT LIKE SOMEONE WHO THINKS MORE ABOUT GARBAGE...

...ABOUT WHAT TRASH I CREATE, AND WHERE IT ENDS UP.

AND THAT'S A START.